SCHIRMER'S LIBRARY
OF MUSICAL CLASSICS

Vol. 1995

ROBERT SCHUMANN

Selected Masterpieces

Vol. 2

For Piano

Edited by
CLARA SCHUMANN

ISBN 0-7935-3066-0

G. SCHIRMER, Inc.

DISTRIBUTED BY

HAL•LEONARD™
CORPORATION
7777 W. BLUEMOUND RD. P.O. BOX 13819 MILWAUKEE, WI 53213

CONTENTS

NOVELETTEN
Novellettes

Edited by Clara Schumann

Robert Schumann, Op. 2
(1838)

Marcato e con forza ♩ = 108

---

*) The Novellettes were at first intended to be inscribed to Chopin, to whom, however, Schumann then dedicated the "Kreisleriana" pieces more akin to his nature.

**) The Trio should be played with full tone, comparable to the rich sound of an alto voice.

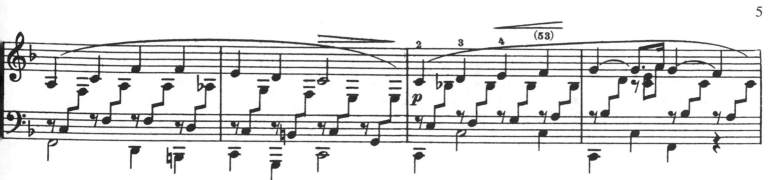

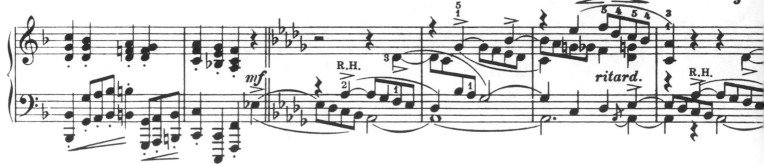

* *Here a softer quality of tone is suitable.*

Most quickly and with bravura ♩= 92

Original version

Intermezzo
Poco più lento, sempre teneramente ♩ = 104

*)
  The ritenuto here has the significance of a "sostenuto" and applies to the whole sequence.

Tempo primo

Original version

Intermezzo
Fast and wild ♩ = 138

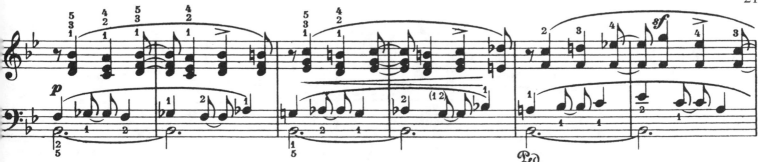

Tempo I

Dance-like, very lively ♩. = 66

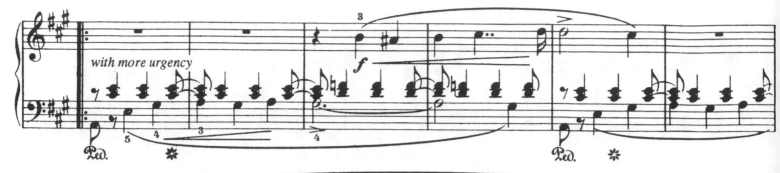

Tempo I

Ancora più mosso

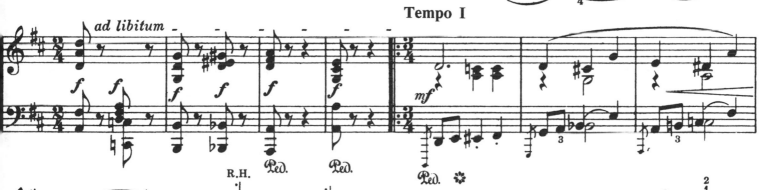

Tempo I

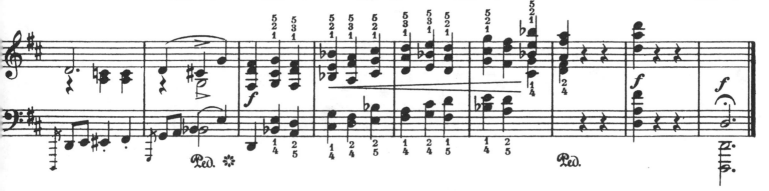

Intoxicating and festive ♩ = 116

5

Un poco più lento

Very lively

Very lively and with much humor ♩=72 *)

6

*) *The tempo, in the course of this piece, must be constantly accelerated*

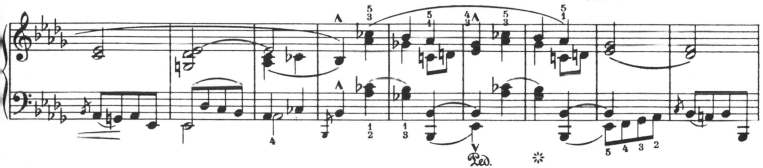

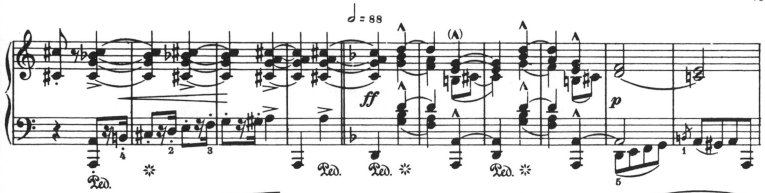

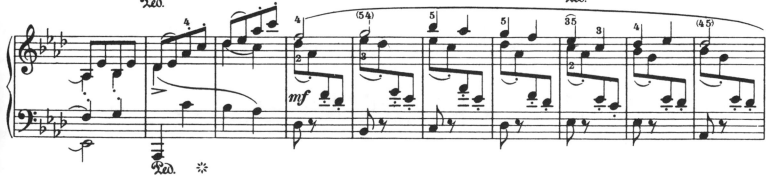

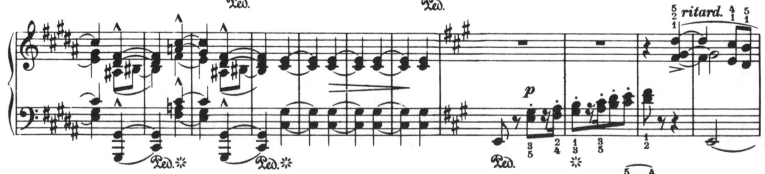

Un poco più lento ♩.=100

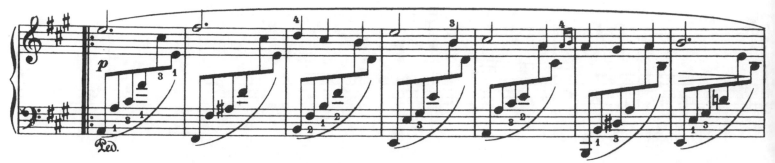

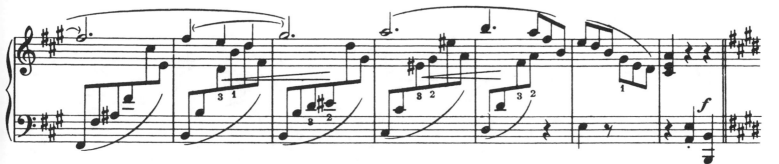

Tempo I

Very lively ♩ = 100

50

Trio I
Still more lively ♩ = 144

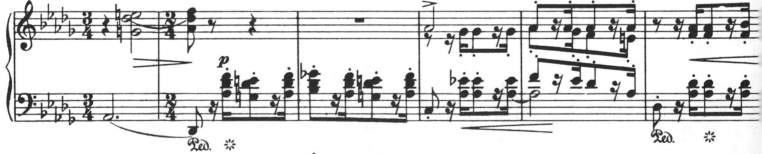

*) *The notes in the left hand are not to be played too short, but with much delicacy and lightness*

As before

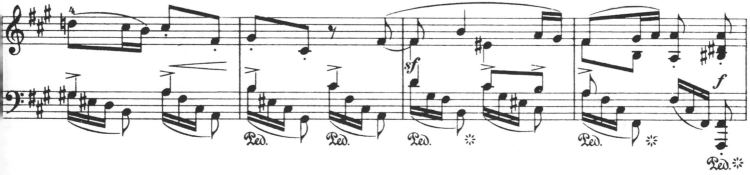

Trio II **Bright and happy** ♩ = 132

Tempo I

A voice from the distance

Continuation

Semplice e cantando ♩ = 96

Adagio

The same tempo as in the previous piece

Adagio

Continuation and end

Lively, not too fast ♩ = 120 *

*) *The tempo becomes increasingly quicker throughout the piece*

More and more lively

With introspection

Tempo I

62

*) *The Adagio here indicates merely an emphasised Rit.*

NACHTSTÜCKE
Night Pieces

Edited by Clara Schumann

1

Rather slow, often restrained ♩ = 100

Robert Schumann, Op. 23
(1839)

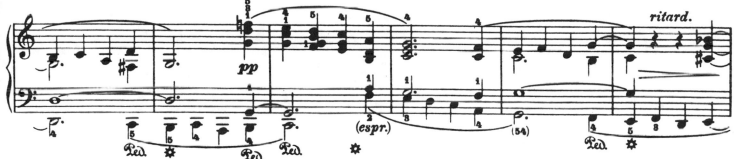

2

Marcato e vivace ♩ = 144

3

With great liveliness ♩. = 76

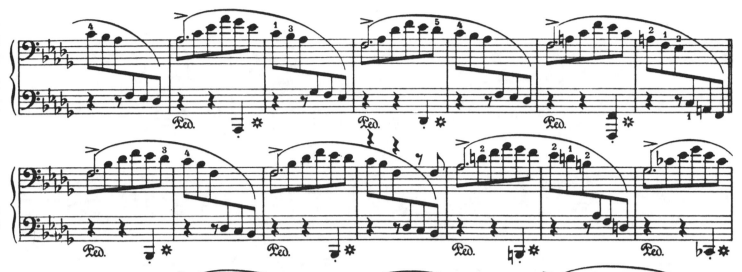

73

Even more lively $\quad \text{♩.} = 92$

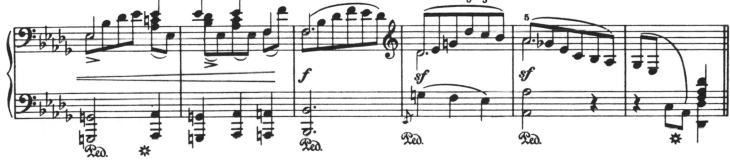

4

Semplice ♩ = 92

*) Played:

dedicated to Mr. Simonin de Sire in Dinant

FASCHINGSSCHWANK AUS WIEN
Imaginary Pictures

Allegro

Robert Schumann, Op.26
(1839)

Tempo I

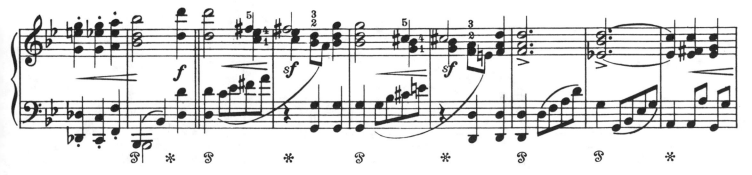

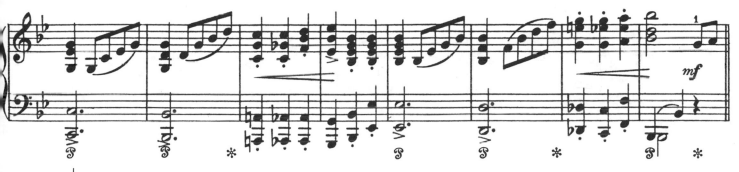

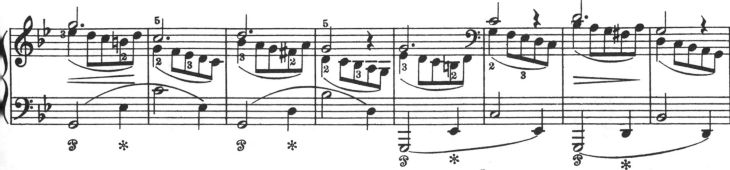

ritard.

Tempo I

short pause

Tempo as before

As lively as possible

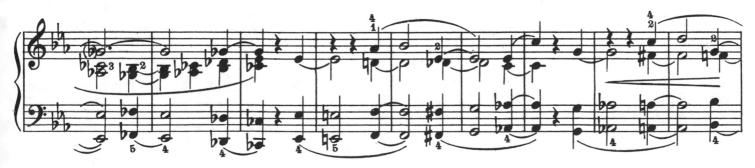

Tempo primo

Coda

Romanze

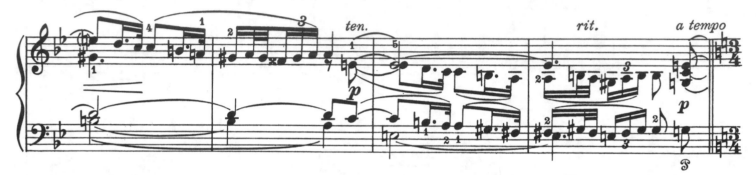

Scherzino

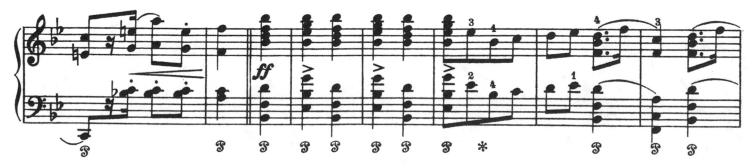

Intermezzo

With the greatest energy ♩ = 116

Ped. sim.

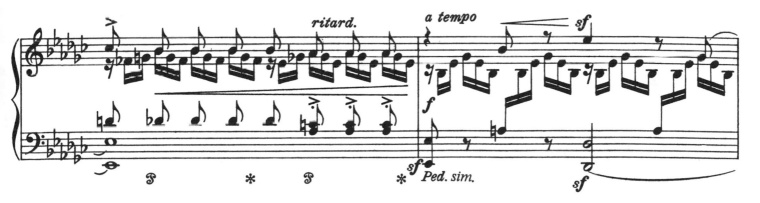

Finale

Most lively ♩ = 138

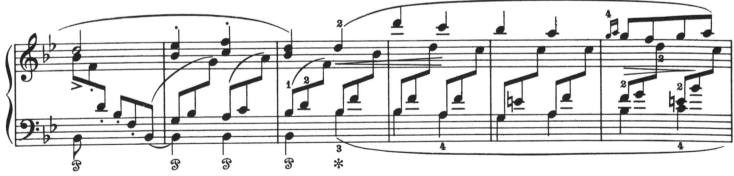

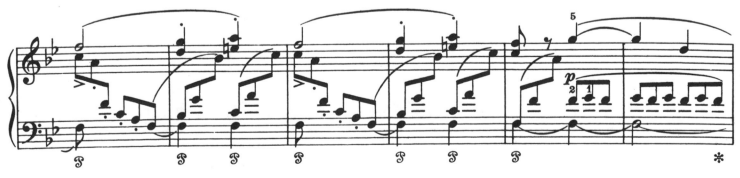

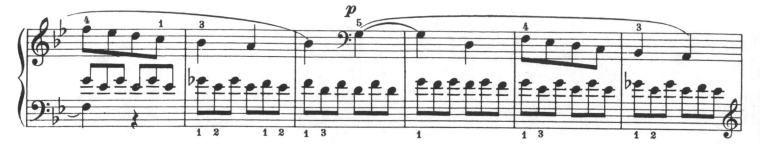

Presto

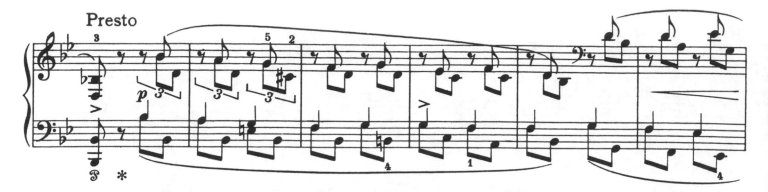

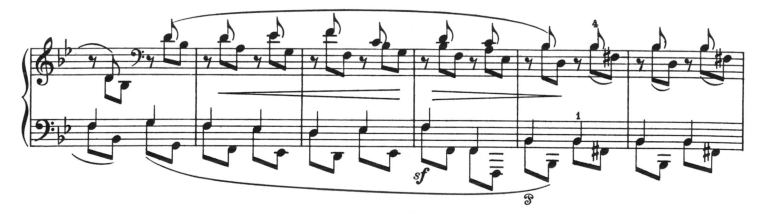

WALDSZENEN
FOREST SCENES
Nine Piano Pieces

Dedicated to Annette Preusser

Robert Schumann, Op. 82
(1848-49)

Entrance

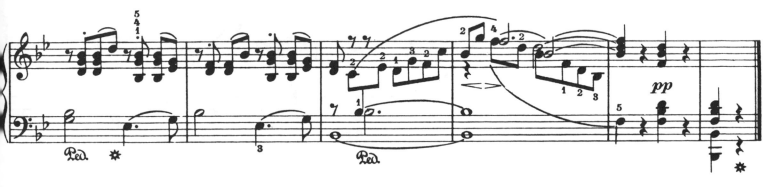

Hunter in Ambush

Lonely Flowers

Semplice ♩=96

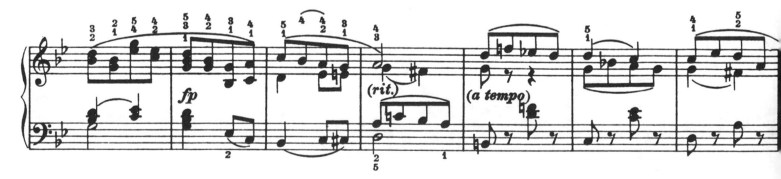

Un poco più mosso

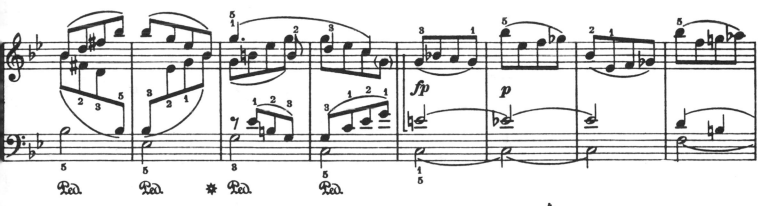

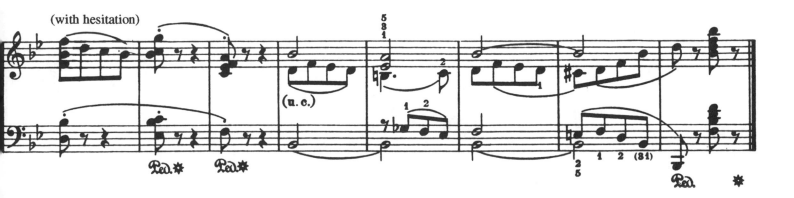

Place of Infamy

The flowers, tall as they are,
Are pale here, as death is pale;
One only, in the center
Stands there in dark red

It doesn't have its color from the sun:
Never was it touched by the sun's glow;
It has its color from the earth,
The earth that drank the blood of men.

F. Hebbel

Rather slowly ♩ = 60

*) *The editor plays the lower grace-notes detached:*

Friendly Landscape

Un poco più lento

In Tempo

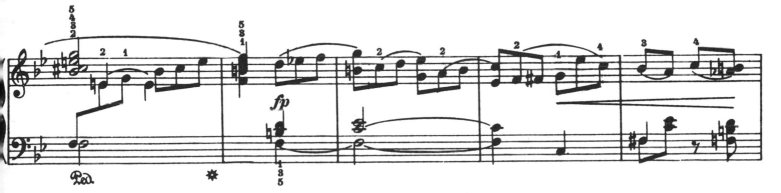

Un poco più lento   **In Tempo**

The Wayside Inn

Un poco ritardando

In tempo

Un poco lento
In tempo

Bird as Prophet

Lento, teneramente assai ♩ = 63

*) *Care should be taken not to over-emphasize the dissonances, (fp) already prominent of themselves; a slight accent is sufficient here.*

Un poco più lento

In tempo

Hunting Song

Fast, forcefully ♩. = 120

The Departure

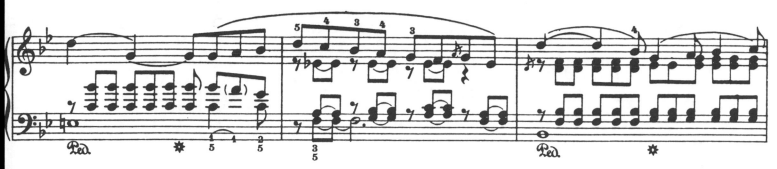

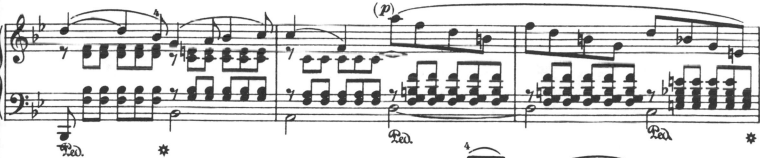

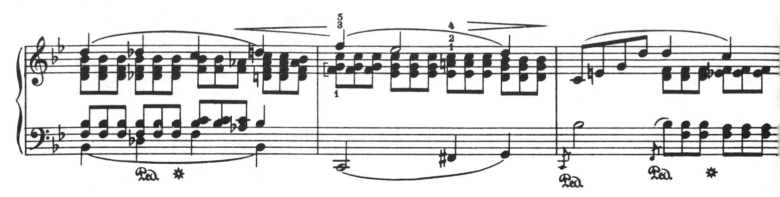

Sempre decrescendo

dedicated to Miss Mary Potts

BUNTE BLÄTTER

Three Little Pieces No. 1

Robert Schumann, Op. 99
(1839)

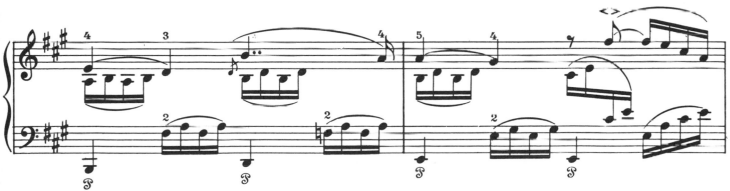

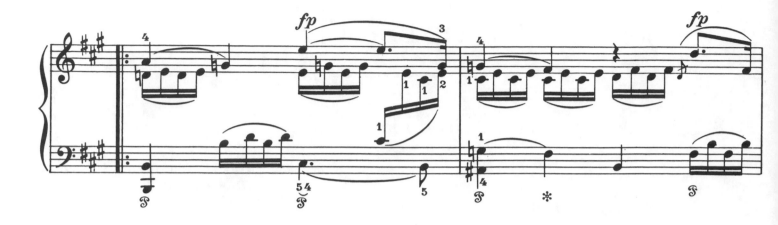

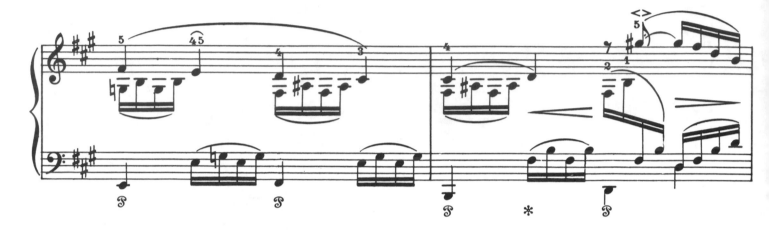

Three Little Pieces No. 2

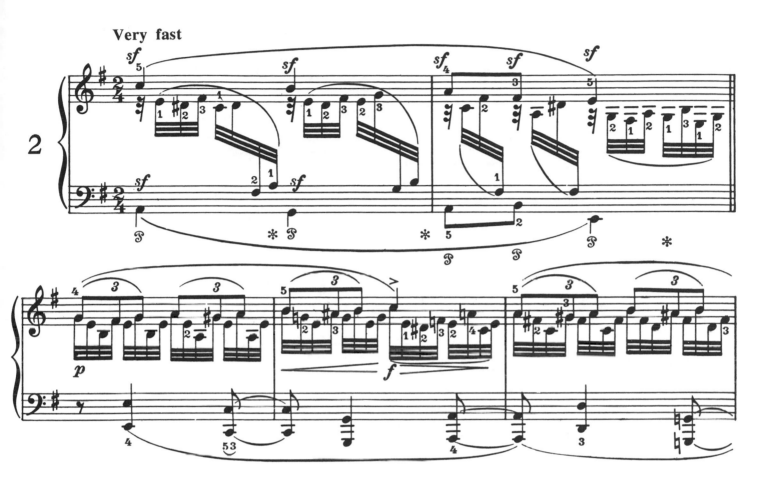

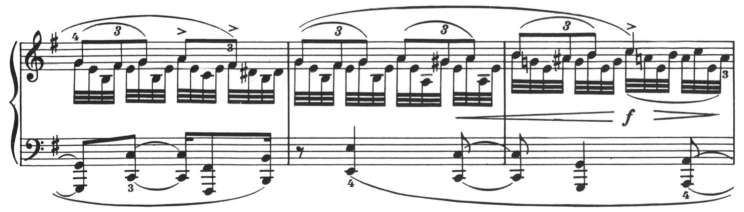

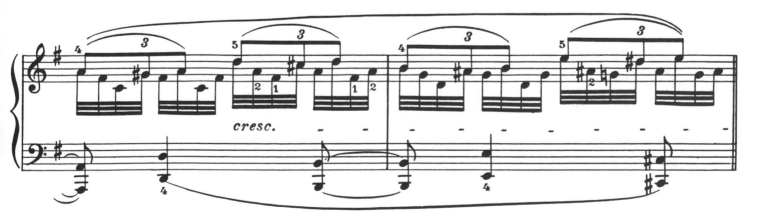

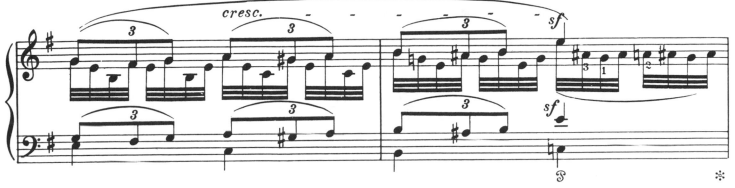

Three Little Pieces No. 3

Album Pages No. 1

(1841)

Rather slowly

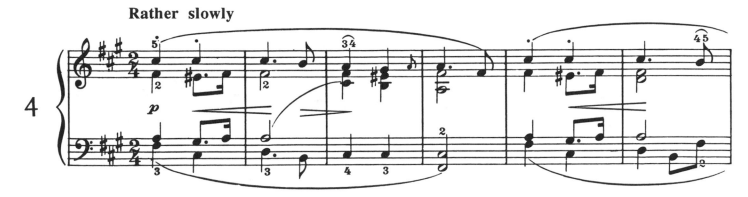

Album Pages No. 2

(1838)

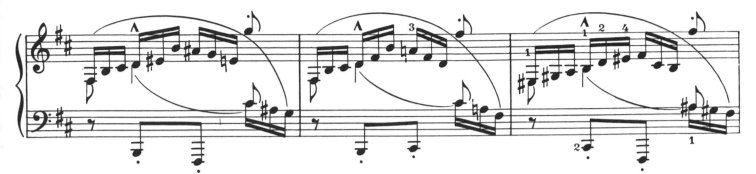

Album Pages No. 3

Rather slow, very songful

(1837)

Album Pages No. 4

(1838)

Album Pages No. 5

(1838)

Novellette

(1838)

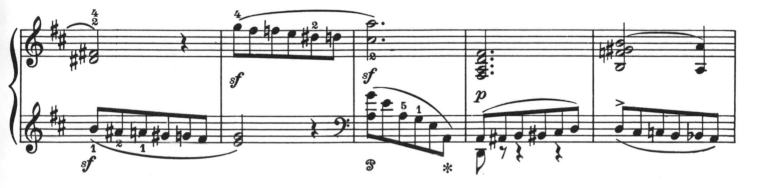

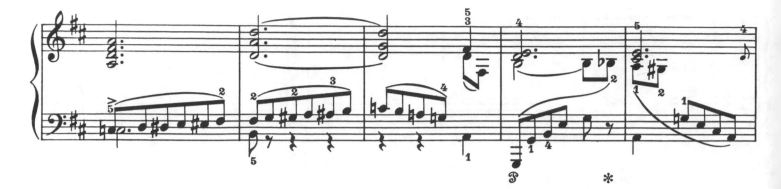

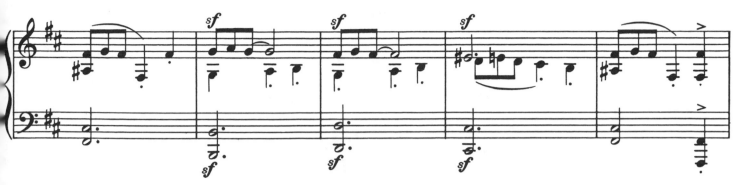

Prelude

(1839)

Energetically

10

150

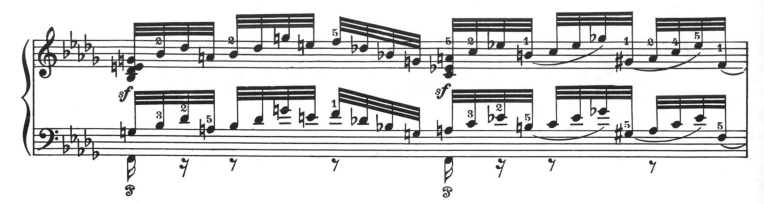

151

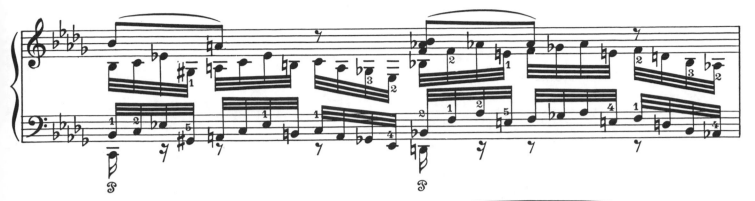

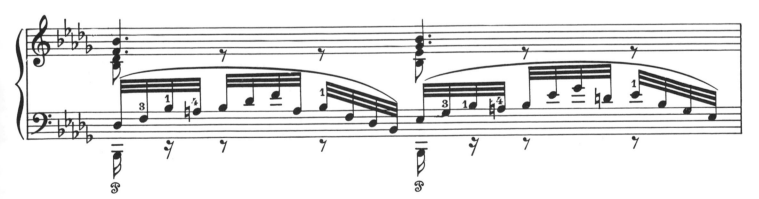

March

(1843)

Molto sostenuto

11

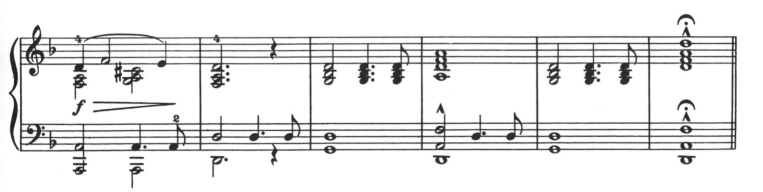

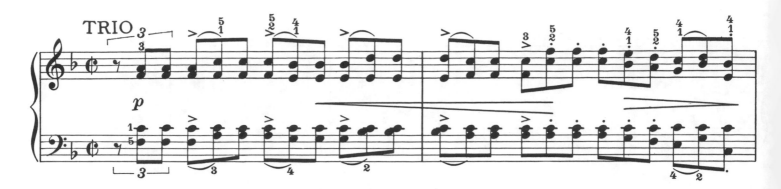

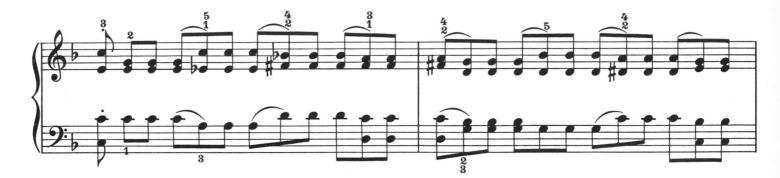

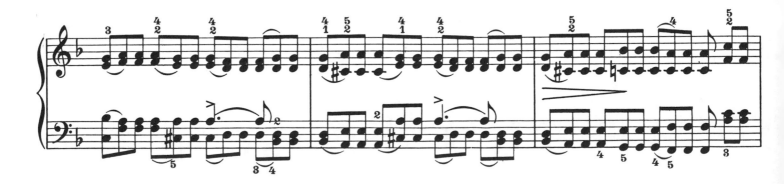

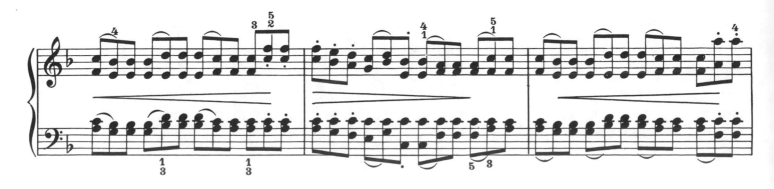

Evening Music

(1841)

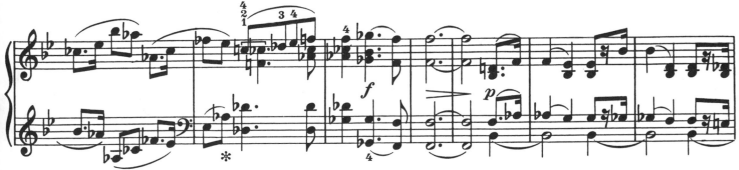

Scherzo

(1841)

13

More lively

Quickstep

Marcato molto

(1849)

14

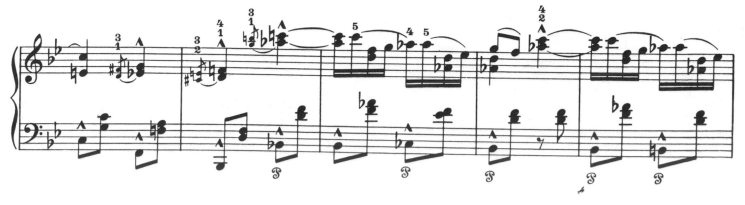

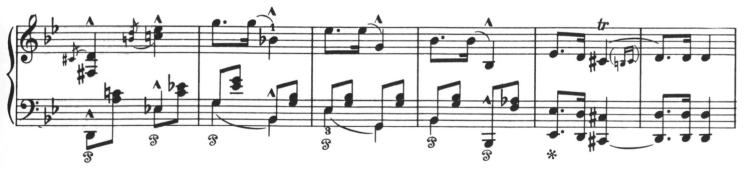

DREI PHANTASIESTÜCKE
Three Fantastic Pieces

Edited by Clara Schumann

Robert Schumann, Op. 111
(1851)

1

Molto vivace ed appassionatamente ♩ = 84

2

Rather slowly ♩ = 72

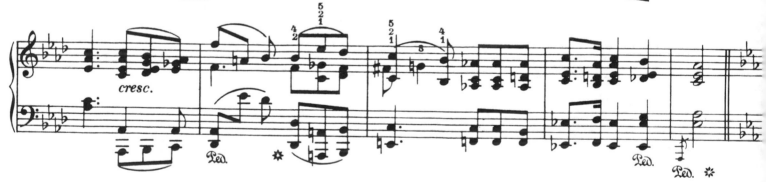

Un poco più mosso

Tempo I

3

Forcefully, and strongly accented ♩ = 96